THE VINTAGE LADIES

IMAGES CURATED
& COPY LINES WRITTEN
BY
MARILYN MESSIK

Copyright © 2021 Marilyn Messik

The moral right of the author has been asserted.

Apart from any fair dealing for the purposes of research or private study, or criticism or review, as permitted under the Copyright Designs and Patents Act 1988, this publication may only be reproduced, stored or transmitted, in any form or by any means with the prior permission in writing of the publisher, or in the case of reprographic reproduction in accordance with the terms of licences issued by the Copyright Licensing Agency. Enquiries concerning reproduction outside those terms, should be sent to the publisher.

First Edition, 2021

VINTAGE LADIES

Vintage Ladies is the publishing arm of Create Communication.

www.createcommunication.co.uk
talk@createcommunication.co.uk
0208 421 3328 ~ 0788 799 5749

A catalogue record for this book is available from the British Library.

Cover: William Morris

Designed and set in the UK by GAIL D'ALMAINE
dalmaine.com

Dedicated to, and celebrating
Lovers of Books, everywhere!

Grateful thanks extended to the Estate of the late Hildegard Boneforte 1870 – 1965, for kind permission to quote from The Sayings of Hildegard Bonefort.

(First Edition 1895)

Also Available in this Series:
The Vintage Ladies Collection. Vol. 1.
The Vintage Ladies Everlasting Diary.
The Vintage Ladies Journal.
The Vintage Ladies Notebook.

Contents

Introduction	5
January	8
February	22
March	36
April	50
May	64
June	78
July	92
August	106
September	120
October	134
November	148
December	162

Dear Fellow Book Lover,

I am beyond delighted this Book Log has found its way into your hands, but how you use it is entirely up to you. When it comes to recording your reading and thoughts you may be a prodigious and dedicated (obsessive?) jotter. On the other hand you could equally well be a 'sometimes I do, sometimes I don't,' kind of a person.

Whether you're a thriller fan, rabidly into romance, or an autobiography addict, and however it suits you to use it, enjoy your Book Lovers Log with all my very best wishes, and I hope the Vintage Ladies put a smile on your face while you do.

Marilyn Messik

PS. I always love to hear from you, drop me a line with your thoughts. marilyn@createcommunication.co.uk

"An excellent book, a box of chocolates and a glass of wine is a rare pleasure. Waiting for someone to suggest it only makes it rarer. Don't wait!"
                    Hildegarde Boneforte (The Hon.) 1870 – 1965

AN HOUR SPENT
IS AN HOUR
SPENT

YOU CAN NEVER
SPEND IT AGAIN.

BUT AN HOUR
SPENT WITH A
GOOD BOOK
IS AN HOUR
SPENT
WELL

When you're reading a brilliant book and can't wait to get back to it.

Mildred has agreed to become Chairwoman at Bookclub, but is a little surprised to find there's a ceremony involved.

Fred's reading Classics at Oxford, and has thrown himself right into it.

BOOKS DURING JANUARY

TITLE:
....

AUTHOR:
....

Book　　Ebook　　Audio　　Series　　Standalone　　New Author

✥ MY THOUGHTS ✥

BOOKS DURING JANUARY

TITLE:
....

AUTHOR:
....

Book ▪   Ebook ▪   Audio ▪   Series ▪   Standalone ▪   New Author ▪

~ MY THOUGHTS ~

BOOKS DURING JANUARY

TITLE:
....

AUTHOR:
....

Book　　Ebook　　Audio　　Series　　Standalone　　New Author

◈ MY THOUGHTS ◈

....
....
....
....
....
....
....
....
....
....
....
....
....
....
....
....
....
....
....
....
....
....

BOOKS DURING JANUARY

TITLE:
....

AUTHOR:
....

Book ▢ Ebook ▢ Audio ▢ Series ▢ Standalone ▢ New Author ▢

～ MY THOUGHTS ～

....
....
....
....
....
....
....
....
....
....
....
....
....
....
....
....
....
....
....
....

BOOKS DURING JANUARY

TITLE:
....
AUTHOR:
....

Book ▪ Ebook ▪ Audio ▪ Series ▪ Standalone ▪ New Author ▪

~ MY THOUGHTS ~

BOOKS DURING JANUARY

TITLE:
....

AUTHOR:
....

Book ☐ Ebook ☐ Audio ☐ Series ☐ Standalone ☐ New Author ☐

~ MY THOUGHTS ~

BOOKS DURING JANUARY

TITLE:
....

AUTHOR:
....

Book ▪ Ebook ▪ Audio ▪ Series ▪ Standalone ▪ New Author

❧ MY THOUGHTS ☙

BOOKS DURING JANUARY

TITLE:
....
AUTHOR:
....

Book ▪ Ebook ▪ Audio ▪ Series ▪ Standalone ▪ New Author

∼ MY THOUGHTS ∼

....
....
....
....
....
....
....
....
....
....
....
....
....
....
....
....
....
....
....

MY JANUARY BOOK REVIEWS

TITLE:

AUTHOR:

DATE OF REVIEW:

Placed On: ☐ Amazon
             ☐ Goodreads
             ☐ Blog
             ☐ Audible
             ☐ Other

My Star Rating   ☆ ☆ ☆ ☆ ☆

TITLE:

AUTHOR:

DATE OF REVIEW:

Placed On: ☐ Amazon
             ☐ Goodreads
             ☐ Blog
             ☐ Audible
             ☐ Other

My Star Rating   ☆ ☆ ☆ ☆ ☆

MY JANUARY BOOK REVIEWS

TITLE:
....

AUTHOR:
....

DATE OF REVIEW:
....

Placed On: ▫ Amazon
             ▫ Goodreads
             ▫ Blog
             ▫ Audible
             ▫ Other

My Star Rating   ☆ ☆ ☆ ☆ ☆

TITLE:
....

AUTHOR:
....

DATE OF REVIEW:
....

Placed On: ▫ Amazon
             ▫ Goodreads
             ▫ Blog
             ▫ Audible
             ▫ Other

My Star Rating   ☆ ☆ ☆ ☆ ☆

MY JANUARY BOOK REVIEWS

TITLE:
....

AUTHOR:
....

DATE OF REVIEW:
....

Placed On: ▪ Amazon
             ▪ Goodreads
             ▪ Blog
             ▪ Audible
             ▪ Other

My Star Rating   ☆ ☆ ☆ ☆ ☆

TITLE:
....

AUTHOR:
....

DATE OF REVIEW:
....

Placed On: ▪ Amazon
             ▪ Goodreads
             ▪ Blog
             ▪ Audible
             ▪ Other

My Star Rating   ☆ ☆ ☆ ☆ ☆

MY JANUARY BOOK REVIEWS

TITLE:
....

AUTHOR:
....

DATE OF REVIEW:
....

Placed On:
- ☐ Amazon
- ☐ Goodreads
- ☐ Blog
- ☐ Audible
- ☐ Other

My Star Rating   ☆ ☆ ☆ ☆ ☆

TITLE:
....

AUTHOR:
....

DATE OF REVIEW:
....

Placed On:
- ☐ Amazon
- ☐ Goodreads
- ☐ Blog
- ☐ Audible
- ☐ Other

My Star Rating   ☆ ☆ ☆ ☆ ☆

Sometimes Fanny wonders whether she's lost the plot. Other times she wonders whether she ever had it in the first place.

Jasmine put her book down for only a moment. Problem is it has a floral cover, she may never find it again.

"Saying 'I've decided to be selfish for once!' is generally a sure indication of quite the opposite!"
Hildegarde Boneforte (The Hon.)

BOOKS DURING FEBRUARY

TITLE:
....

AUTHOR:
....

Book   Ebook   Audio   Series   Standalone   New Author

✎ MY THOUGHTS ✎

BOOKS DURING FEBRUARY

TITLE:
....

AUTHOR:
....

Book ▪ Ebook ▪ Audio ▪ Series ▪ Standalone ▪ New Author

⤜ MY THOUGHTS ⤛

BOOKS DURING FEBRUARY

TITLE:
....

AUTHOR:
....

Book ▪ Ebook ▪ Audio ▪ Series ▪ Standalone ▪ New Author ▪

~ MY THOUGHTS ~

....
....
....
....
....
....
....
....
....
....
....
....
....
....
....
....
....
....
....
....
....
....
....

BOOKS DURING FEBRUARY

TITLE:
....

AUTHOR:
....

Book   Ebook   Audio   Series   Standalone   New Author

~ MY THOUGHTS ~

BOOKS DURING FEBRUARY

TITLE:
....

AUTHOR:
....

Book ▪ Ebook ▪ Audio ▪ Series ▪ Standalone ▪ New Author

~ MY THOUGHTS ~

BOOKS DURING FEBRUARY

TITLE:

AUTHOR:

Book   Ebook   Audio   Series   Standalone   New Author

~ MY THOUGHTS ~

BOOKS DURING FEBRUARY

TITLE:
....

AUTHOR:
....

Book ▫ Ebook ▫ Audio ▫ Series ▫ Standalone ▫ New Author

～ MY THOUGHTS ～

BOOKS DURING FEBRUARY

TITLE:
....

AUTHOR:
....

Book   Ebook   Audio   Series   Standalone   New Author

~ MY THOUGHTS ~

....
....
....
....
....
....
....
....
....
....
....
....
....
....
....
....
....
....
....
....

MY FEBRUARY BOOK REVIEWS

TITLE:

AUTHOR:

DATE OF REVIEW:

Placed On:
- Amazon
- Goodreads
- Blog
- Audible
- Other

My Star Rating ☆ ☆ ☆ ☆

TITLE:

AUTHOR:

DATE OF REVIEW:

Placed On:
- Amazon
- Goodreads
- Blog
- Audible
- Other

My Star Rating ☆ ☆ ☆ ☆

MY FEBRUARY BOOK REVIEWS

TITLE:
....

AUTHOR:
....

DATE OF REVIEW:
....

Placed On:
- ☐ Amazon
- ☐ Goodreads
- ☐ Blog
- ☐ Audible
- ☐ Other

My Star Rating ☆ ☆ ☆ ☆ ☆

TITLE:
....

AUTHOR:
....

DATE OF REVIEW:
....

Placed On:
- ☐ Amazon
- ☐ Goodreads
- ☐ Blog
- ☐ Audible
- ☐ Other

My Star Rating ☆ ☆ ☆ ☆ ☆

MY FEBRUARY BOOK REVIEWS

TITLE:
....

AUTHOR:
....

DATE OF REVIEW:
....

Placed On:
- Amazon
- Goodreads
- Blog
- Audible
- Other

My Star Rating ☆ ☆ ☆ ☆ ☆

TITLE:
....

AUTHOR:
....

DATE OF REVIEW:
....

Placed On:
- Amazon
- Goodreads
- Blog
- Audible
- Other

My Star Rating ☆ ☆ ☆ ☆ ☆

MY FEBRUARY BOOK REVIEWS

TITLE: ....

AUTHOR: ....

DATE OF REVIEW: ....

Placed On: ☐ Amazon
            ☐ Goodreads
            ☐ Blog
            ☐ Audible
            ☐ Other

My Star Rating   ☆ ☆ ☆ ☆ ☆

TITLE: ....

AUTHOR: ....

DATE OF REVIEW: ....

Placed On: ☐ Amazon
            ☐ Goodreads
            ☐ Blog
            ☐ Audible
            ☐ Other

My Star Rating   ☆ ☆ ☆ ☆ ☆

Dorothea is extremely surprised by what Lady C. does next!

Saphira has just this moment finished the latest Mills & Boon, and is feeling a little wrung out.

"There's only one thing more tiring than being a pessimist, and that's being an imaginative pessimist."
Hildegarde Boneforte (The Hon.)

BOOKS DURING MARCH

TITLE:
....

AUTHOR:
....

Book ▪ Ebook ▪ Audio ▪ Series ▪ Standalone ▪ New Author

✎ MY THOUGHTS ✎

....
....
....
....
....
....
....
....
....
....
....
....
....
....
....
....
....
....
....
....
....

BOOKS DURING MARCH

TITLE:
....
AUTHOR:
....

Book ▪ Ebook ▪ Audio ▪ Series ▪ Standalone ▪ New Author ▪

~ MY THOUGHTS ~

BOOKS DURING MARCH

TITLE:
....

AUTHOR:
....

Book ▫   Ebook ▫   Audio ▫   Series ▫   Standalone ▫   New Author ▫

~ MY THOUGHTS ~

....
....
....
....
....
....
....
....
....
....
....
....
....
....
....
....
....
....
....
....
....
....

BOOKS DURING MARCH

TITLE:
....

AUTHOR:
....

Book ▪ Ebook ▪ Audio ▪ Series ▪ Standalone ▪ New Author ▪

☙ MY THOUGHTS ☙

....
....
....
....
....
....
....
....
....
....
....
....
....
....
....
....
....
....
....
....

BOOKS DURING MARCH

TITLE:
....

AUTHOR:
....

Book   Ebook   Audio   Series   Standalone   New Author

~ MY THOUGHTS ~

BOOKS DURING MARCH

TITLE: ....

AUTHOR: ....

Book ▪ Ebook ▪ Audio ▪ Series ▪ Standalone ▪ New Author

～ MY THOUGHTS ～

BOOKS DURING MARCH

TITLE:
....

AUTHOR:
....

Book   Ebook   Audio   Series   Standalone   New Author

~ MY THOUGHTS ~

....
....
....
....
....
....
....
....
....
....
....
....
....
....
....
....
....
....
....
....
....
....
....
....

BOOKS DURING MARCH

TITLE:
....

AUTHOR:
....

Book   Ebook   Audio   Series   Standalone   New Author

✶ MY THOUGHTS ✶

MY MARCH BOOK REVIEWS

TITLE:

AUTHOR:

DATE OF REVIEW:

Placed On:
- [ ] Amazon
- [ ] Goodreads
- [ ] Blog
- [ ] Audible
- [ ] Other

My Star Rating   ☆ ☆ ☆ ☆

TITLE:

AUTHOR:

DATE OF REVIEW:

Placed On:
- [ ] Amazon
- [ ] Goodreads
- [ ] Blog
- [ ] Audible
- [ ] Other

My Star Rating   ☆ ☆ ☆ ☆

MY MARCH BOOK REVIEWS

TITLE:
....

AUTHOR:
....

DATE OF REVIEW:
....

Placed On:
- Amazon
- Goodreads
- Blog
- Audible
- Other

My Star Rating ☆ ☆ ☆ ☆ ☆

TITLE:
....

AUTHOR:
....

DATE OF REVIEW:
....

Placed On:
- Amazon
- Goodreads
- Blog
- Audible
- Other

My Star Rating ☆ ☆ ☆ ☆ ☆

MY MARCH BOOK REVIEWS

TITLE:
....
AUTHOR:
....
DATE OF REVIEW:
....

Placed On:
- Amazon
- Goodreads
- Blog
- Audible
- Other

My Star Rating ☆ ☆ ☆ ☆ ☆

TITLE:
....
AUTHOR:
....
DATE OF REVIEW:
....

Placed On:
- Amazon
- Goodreads
- Blog
- Audible
- Other

My Star Rating ☆ ☆ ☆ ☆ ☆

MY MARCH BOOK REVIEWS

TITLE:
....

AUTHOR:
....

DATE OF REVIEW:
....

Placed On: ☐ Amazon
             ☐ Goodreads
             ☐ Blog
             ☐ Audible
             ☐ Other

My Star Rating   ☆ ☆ ☆ ☆ ☆

TITLE:
....

AUTHOR:
....

DATE OF REVIEW:
....

Placed On: ☐ Amazon
             ☐ Goodreads
             ☐ Blog
             ☐ Audible
             ☐ Other

My Star Rating   ☆ ☆ ☆ ☆ ☆

Alicia's just found the sequel isn't coming out until next year.

Conrad tends to have
a firm opinion
on most things.

*"Never shut the door on a window
of opportunity."*
Hildegarde Boneforte (The Hon.)

BOOKS DURING APRIL

TITLE:
....

AUTHOR:
....

Book ▢   Ebook ▢   Audio ▢   Series ▢   Standalone ▢   New Author ▢

✦ MY THOUGHTS ✦

....
....
....
....
....
....
....
....
....
....
....
....
....
....
....
....
....
....
....
....

BOOKS DURING APRIL

TITLE:

AUTHOR:

Book   Ebook   Audio   Series   Standalone   New Author

~ MY THOUGHTS ~

BOOKS DURING APRIL

TITLE:
....

AUTHOR:
....

Book ▫ Ebook ▫ Audio ▫ Series ▫ Standalone ▫ New Author

⋙ MY THOUGHTS ⋘

BOOKS DURING APRIL

TITLE:

AUTHOR:

Book   Ebook   Audio   Series   Standalone   New Author

MY THOUGHTS

BOOKS DURING APRIL

TITLE:
....

AUTHOR:
....

Book ▢ Ebook ▢ Audio ▢ Series ▢ Standalone ▢ New Author ▢

~ MY THOUGHTS ~

BOOKS DURING APRIL

TITLE:
....

AUTHOR:
....

Book　　Ebook　　Audio　　Series　　Standalone　　New Author

⥈ MY THOUGHTS ⥊

BOOKS DURING APRIL

TITLE:
....

AUTHOR:
....

Book   Ebook   Audio   Series   Standalone   New Author

～ MY THOUGHTS ～

....
....
....
....
....
....
....
....
....
....
....
....
....
....
....
....
....
....
....
....
....

BOOKS DURING APRIL

TITLE:
....

AUTHOR:
....

Book   Ebook   Audio   Series   Standalone   New Author

MY THOUGHTS

MY APRIL BOOK REVIEWS

TITLE:
....

AUTHOR:
....

DATE OF REVIEW:
....

Placed On:	▪ Amazon
	▪ Goodreads
	▪ Blog
	▪ Audible
	▪ Other

My Star Rating	☆ ☆ ☆ ☆ ☆

TITLE:
....

AUTHOR:
....

DATE OF REVIEW:
....

Placed On:	▪ Amazon
	▪ Goodreads
	▪ Blog
	▪ Audible
	▪ Other

My Star Rating	☆ ☆ ☆ ☆ ☆

MY APRIL BOOK REVIEWS

TITLE:
....

AUTHOR:
....

DATE OF REVIEW:
....

Placed On:　　☐ Amazon
　　　　　　　☐ Goodreads
　　　　　　　☐ Blog
　　　　　　　☐ Audible
　　　　　　　☐ Other

My Star Rating　　☆ ☆ ☆ ☆ ☆

TITLE:
....

AUTHOR:
....

DATE OF REVIEW:
....

Placed On:　　☐ Amazon
　　　　　　　☐ Goodreads
　　　　　　　☐ Blog
　　　　　　　☐ Audible
　　　　　　　☐ Other

My Star Rating　　☆ ☆ ☆ ☆ ☆

MY APRIL BOOK REVIEWS

TITLE:
....
AUTHOR:
....
DATE OF REVIEW:
....

Placed On: ▪ Amazon
             ▪ Goodreads
             ▪ Blog
             ▪ Audible
             ▪ Other

My Star Rating   ☆ ☆ ☆ ☆ ☆

TITLE:
....
AUTHOR:
....
DATE OF REVIEW:
....

Placed On: ▪ Amazon
             ▪ Goodreads
             ▪ Blog
             ▪ Audible
             ▪ Other

My Star Rating   ☆ ☆ ☆ ☆ ☆

MY APRIL BOOK REVIEWS

TITLE:
....

AUTHOR:
....

DATE OF REVIEW:
....

Placed On: ☐ Amazon
             ☐ Goodreads
             ☐ Blog
             ☐ Audible
             ☐ Other

My Star Rating   ☆ ☆ ☆ ☆ ☆

TITLE:
....

AUTHOR:
....

DATE OF REVIEW:
....

Placed On: ☐ Amazon
             ☐ Goodreads
             ☐ Blog
             ☐ Audible
             ☐ Other

My Star Rating   ☆ ☆ ☆ ☆ ☆

Discussion was held as to who should be Frank and who should be Earnest.

Once a year, the Friends of Jane Austen club members like to let their hair down.

"Shutting your eyes to things won't take a weight off your mind."
Hildegarde Boneforte (The Hon.)

BOOKS DURING MAY

TITLE:
....

AUTHOR:
....

Book   Ebook   Audio   Series   Standalone   New Author

❧ MY THOUGHTS ☙

BOOKS DURING MAY

TITLE:

AUTHOR:

Book   Ebook   Audio   Series   Standalone   New Author

MY THOUGHTS

BOOKS DURING MAY

TITLE:
....

AUTHOR:
....

Book　　Ebook　　Audio　　Series　　Standalone　　New Author

～ MY THOUGHTS ～

BOOKS DURING MAY

TITLE:
....

AUTHOR:
....

Book　　Ebook　　Audio　　Series　　Standalone　　New Author

☙ MY THOUGHTS ☙

BOOKS DURING MAY

TITLE:
....

AUTHOR:
....

Book ☐   Ebook ☐   Audio ☐   Series ☐   Standalone ☐   New Author ☐

⚜ MY THOUGHTS ⚜

BOOKS DURING MAY

TITLE: ....

AUTHOR: ....

Book ▮ Ebook ▮ Audio ▮ Series ▮ Standalone ▮ New Author ▮

⤛ MY THOUGHTS ⤜

....
....
....
....
....
....
....
....
....
....
....
....
....
....
....
....
....
....
....

BOOKS DURING MAY

TITLE:
....

AUTHOR:
....

Book ▪ Ebook ▪ Audio ▪ Series ▪ Standalone ▪ New Author ▪

～ MY THOUGHTS ～

BOOKS DURING MAY

TITLE: ....

AUTHOR: ....

Book ▪ Ebook ▪ Audio ▪ Series ▪ Standalone ▪ New Author ▪

❧ MY THOUGHTS ☙

MY MAY BOOK REVIEWS

TITLE:
....

AUTHOR:
....

DATE OF REVIEW:
....

Placed On: ▪ Amazon
              ▪ Goodreads
              ▪ Blog
              ▪ Audible
              ▪ Other

My Star Rating   ☆ ☆ ☆ ☆ ☆

TITLE:
....

AUTHOR:
....

DATE OF REVIEW:
....

Placed On: ▪ Amazon
              ▪ Goodreads
              ▪ Blog
              ▪ Audible
              ▪ Other

My Star Rating   ☆ ☆ ☆ ☆ ☆

MY MAY BOOK REVIEWS

TITLE:

AUTHOR:

DATE OF REVIEW:

Placed On: ☐ Amazon
             ☐ Goodreads
             ☐ Blog
             ☐ Audible
             ☐ Other

My Star Rating   ☆ ☆ ☆ ☆ ☆

TITLE:

AUTHOR:

DATE OF REVIEW:

Placed On: ☐ Amazon
             ☐ Goodreads
             ☐ Blog
             ☐ Audible
             ☐ Other

My Star Rating   ☆ ☆ ☆ ☆ ☆

MY MAY BOOK REVIEWS

TITLE:
....
AUTHOR:
....
DATE OF REVIEW:
....

Placed On: ▪ Amazon
             ▪ Goodreads
             ▪ Blog
             ▪ Audible
             ▪ Other

My Star Rating   ☆ ☆ ☆ ☆ ☆

TITLE:
....
AUTHOR:
....
DATE OF REVIEW:
....

Placed On: ▪ Amazon
             ▪ Goodreads
             ▪ Blog
             ▪ Audible
             ▪ Other

My Star Rating   ☆ ☆ ☆ ☆ ☆

MY MAY BOOK REVIEWS

TITLE:
....

AUTHOR:
....

DATE OF REVIEW:
....

Placed On: ▫ Amazon
             ▫ Goodreads
             ▫ Blog
             ▫ Audible
             ▫ Other

My Star Rating   ☆ ☆ ☆ ☆ ☆

TITLE:
....

AUTHOR:
....

DATE OF REVIEW:
....

Placed On: ▫ Amazon
             ▫ Goodreads
             ▫ Blog
             ▫ Audible
             ▫ Other

My Star Rating   ☆ ☆ ☆ ☆ ☆

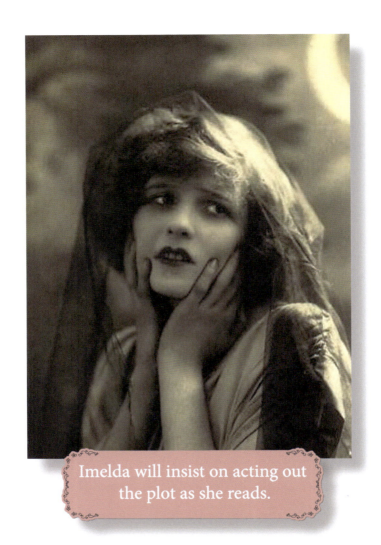

Imelda will insist on acting out the plot as she reads.

"Life is constantly putting out a foot to trip you, the wary are always ready to side-step."
Hildegarde Boneforte (The Hon.)

Elspeth's just finished Daphne Du Maurier's The Birds, and she's taking no chances, the budgie has to go.

BOOKS DURING JUNE

TITLE:

AUTHOR:

Book   Ebook   Audio   Series   Standalone   New Author

✎ MY THOUGHTS ✎

BOOKS DURING JUNE

TITLE:
....

AUTHOR:
....

Book ▪ Ebook ▪ Audio ▪ Series ▪ Standalone ▪ New Author ▪

⇜ MY THOUGHTS ⇝

BOOKS DURING JUNE

TITLE:
....

AUTHOR:
....

Book   Ebook   Audio   Series   Standalone   New Author

✎ MY THOUGHTS ✎

....
....
....
....
....
....
....
....
....
....
....
....
....
....
....
....
....
....
....
....
....
....
....
....

BOOKS DURING JUNE

TITLE:
....
AUTHOR:
....

Book ▪ Ebook ▪ Audio ▪ Series ▪ Standalone ▪ New Author

MY THOUGHTS

BOOKS DURING JUNE

TITLE:
....

AUTHOR:
....

Book   Ebook   Audio   Series   Standalone   New Author

✑ MY THOUGHTS ✑

....
....
....
....
....
....
....
....
....
....
....
....
....
....
....
....
....
....
....
....
....
....
....
....
....
....
....
....

BOOKS DURING JUNE

TITLE:
....

AUTHOR:
....

Book ▫ Ebook ▫ Audio ▫ Series ▫ Standalone ▫ New Author ▫

❧ MY THOUGHTS ❧

BOOKS DURING JUNE

TITLE:
....

AUTHOR:
....

Book   Ebook   Audio   Series   Standalone   New Author

✎ MY THOUGHTS ✎

....
....
....
....
....
....
....
....
....
....
....
....
....
....
....
....
....
....
....
....
....

BOOKS DURING JUNE

TITLE: ....

AUTHOR: ....

Book ▪ Ebook ▪ Audio ▪ Series ▪ Standalone ▪ New Author

⇨ MY THOUGHTS ⇦

MY JUNE BOOK REVIEWS

TITLE:
....
AUTHOR:
....
DATE OF REVIEW:
....

Placed On:
- Amazon
- Goodreads
- Blog
- Audible
- Other

My Star Rating ☆ ☆ ☆ ☆ ☆

TITLE:
....
AUTHOR:
....
DATE OF REVIEW:
....

Placed On:
- Amazon
- Goodreads
- Blog
- Audible
- Other

My Star Rating ☆ ☆ ☆ ☆ ☆

MY JUNE BOOK REVIEWS

TITLE:
....

AUTHOR:
....

DATE OF REVIEW:
....

Placed On: ☐ Amazon
            ☐ Goodreads
            ☐ Blog
            ☐ Audible
            ☐ Other

My Star Rating   ☆ ☆ ☆ ☆ ☆

TITLE:
....

AUTHOR:
....

DATE OF REVIEW:
....

Placed On: ☐ Amazon
            ☐ Goodreads
            ☐ Blog
            ☐ Audible
            ☐ Other

My Star Rating   ☆ ☆ ☆ ☆ ☆

MY JUNE BOOK REVIEWS

TITLE:
....

AUTHOR:
....

DATE OF REVIEW:
....

Placed On: ▢ Amazon
▢ Goodreads
▢ Blog
▢ Audible
▢ Other

My Star Rating   ☆ ☆ ☆ ☆ ☆

TITLE:
....

AUTHOR:
....

DATE OF REVIEW:
....

Placed On: ▢ Amazon
▢ Goodreads
▢ Blog
▢ Audible
▢ Other

My Star Rating   ☆ ☆ ☆ ☆ ☆

MY JUNE BOOK REVIEWS

TITLE:

AUTHOR:

DATE OF REVIEW:

Placed On:
- ☐ Amazon
- ☐ Goodreads
- ☐ Blog
- ☐ Audible
- ☐ Other

My Star Rating   ☆ ☆ ☆ ☆ ☆

TITLE:

AUTHOR:

DATE OF REVIEW:

Placed On:
- ☐ Amazon
- ☐ Goodreads
- ☐ Blog
- ☐ Audible
- ☐ Other

My Star Rating   ☆ ☆ ☆ ☆ ☆

Ermintrude likes to engage fully with a book. She's currently in the middle of Anna Karenina.

"When offspring reach teenage years it is best to lower expectation of communication and recommended you adapt to theirs, a grunt, a groan or an eye-roll ."
Hildegarde Boneforte (The Hon.)

Mother explains gently that if she has to read the ruddy book one more time, she might go completely and permanently round the bend.

BOOKS DURING JULY

TITLE:
....

AUTHOR:
....

Book ▪ Ebook ▪ Audio ▪ Series ▪ Standalone ▪ New Author

⌘ MY THOUGHTS ⌘

BOOKS DURING JULY

TITLE:
....

AUTHOR:
....

Book   Ebook   Audio   Series   Standalone   New Author

❦ MY THOUGHTS ❦

BOOKS DURING JULY

TITLE:
....

AUTHOR:
....

Book Ebook Audio Series Standalone New Author

～ MY THOUGHTS ～

BOOKS DURING JULY

TITLE:
....

AUTHOR:
....

Book ▪ Ebook ▪ Audio ▪ Series ▪ Standalone ▪ New Author ▪

✦ MY THOUGHTS ✦

BOOKS DURING JULY

TITLE:
....

AUTHOR:
....

Book   Ebook   Audio   Series   Standalone   New Author

❦ MY THOUGHTS ❦

....
....
....
....
....
....
....
....
....
....
....
....
....
....
....
....
....
....
....
....
....
....

BOOKS DURING JULY

TITLE:

AUTHOR:

Book   Ebook   Audio   Series   Standalone   New Author

MY THOUGHTS

BOOKS DURING JULY

TITLE:
....

AUTHOR:
....

Book ▪ Ebook ▪ Audio ▪ Series ▪ Standalone ▪ New Author

⌘ MY THOUGHTS ⌘

BOOKS DURING JULY

TITLE:
....

AUTHOR:
....

Book ▪ Ebook ▪ Audio ▪ Series ▪ Standalone ▪ New Author ▪

～ MY THOUGHTS ～

MY JULY BOOK REVIEWS

TITLE:
....

AUTHOR:
....

DATE OF REVIEW:
....

Placed On: ▢ Amazon
             ▢ Goodreads
             ▢ Blog
             ▢ Audible
             ▢ Other

My Star Rating   ☆ ☆ ☆ ☆ ☆

TITLE:
....

AUTHOR:
....

DATE OF REVIEW:
....

Placed On: ▢ Amazon
             ▢ Goodreads
             ▢ Blog
             ▢ Audible
             ▢ Other

My Star Rating   ☆ ☆ ☆ ☆ ☆

MY JULY BOOK REVIEWS

TITLE:

AUTHOR:

DATE OF REVIEW:

Placed On: ☐ Amazon
                 ☐ Goodreads
                 ☐ Blog
                 ☐ Audible
                 ☐ Other

My Star Rating   ☆ ☆ ☆ ☆ ☆

TITLE:

AUTHOR:

DATE OF REVIEW:

Placed On: ☐ Amazon
                 ☐ Goodreads
                 ☐ Blog
                 ☐ Audible
                 ☐ Other

My Star Rating   ☆ ☆ ☆ ☆ ☆

MY JULY BOOK REVIEWS

TITLE:
....
AUTHOR:
....
DATE OF REVIEW:
....

Placed On:	☐ Amazon
	☐ Goodreads
	☐ Blog
	☐ Audible
	☐ Other

My Star Rating	☆ ☆ ☆ ☆ ☆

TITLE:
....
AUTHOR:
....
DATE OF REVIEW:
....

Placed On:	☐ Amazon
	☐ Goodreads
	☐ Blog
	☐ Audible
	☐ Other

My Star Rating	☆ ☆ ☆ ☆ ☆

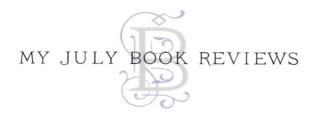

MY JULY BOOK REVIEWS

TITLE:
....

AUTHOR:
....

DATE OF REVIEW:
....

Placed On: ▪ Amazon
            ▪ Goodreads
            ▪ Blog
            ▪ Audible
            ▪ Other

My Star Rating   ☆ ☆ ☆ ☆ ☆

TITLE:
....

AUTHOR:
....

DATE OF REVIEW:
....

Placed On: ▪ Amazon
            ▪ Goodreads
            ▪ Blog
            ▪ Audible
            ▪ Other

My Star Rating   ☆ ☆ ☆ ☆ ☆

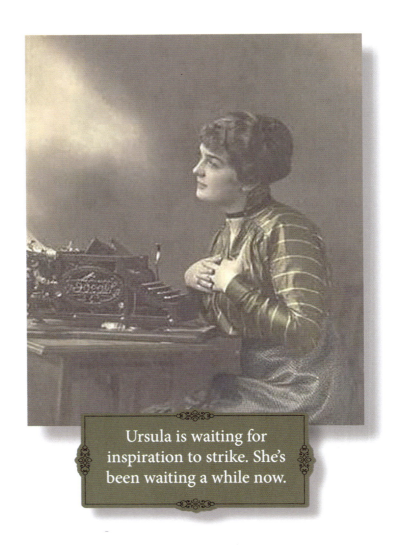

Ursula is waiting for inspiration to strike. She's been waiting a while now.

*"Empathy is an asset.
Great empathy can be a pain."*
Hildegarde Boneforte (The Hon.)

It appears Hilda might have overdosed on Harry Potter.

BOOKS DURING AUGUST

TITLE:
....

AUTHOR:
....

Book   Ebook   Audio   Series   Standalone   New Author

✤ MY THOUGHTS ✤

BOOKS DURING AUGUST

TITLE:
....

AUTHOR:
....

Book ■ Ebook ■ Audio ■ Series ■ Standalone ■ New Author ■

~ MY THOUGHTS ~

BOOKS DURING AUGUST

TITLE:
....

AUTHOR:
....

Book ■ Ebook ■ Audio ■ Series ■ Standalone ■ New Author

❦ MY THOUGHTS ❧

BOOKS DURING AUGUST

TITLE:
....

AUTHOR:
....

Book   Ebook   Audio   Series   Standalone   New Author

~ MY THOUGHTS ~

BOOKS DURING AUGUST

TITLE:

AUTHOR:

Book   Ebook   Audio   Series   Standalone   New Author

MY THOUGHTS

BOOKS DURING AUGUST

TITLE:
....

AUTHOR:
....

Book   Ebook   Audio   Series   Standalone   New Author

✎ MY THOUGHTS ✎

BOOKS DURING AUGUST

TITLE:
....

AUTHOR:
....

Book ▪ Ebook ▪ Audio ▪ Series ▪ Standalone ▪ New Author ▪

✤ MY THOUGHTS ✤

BOOKS DURING AUGUST

TITLE: ....

AUTHOR: ....

Book   Ebook   Audio   Series   Standalone   New Author

❦ MY THOUGHTS ❦

MY AUGUST BOOK REVIEWS

TITLE:
....

AUTHOR:
....

DATE OF REVIEW:
....

Placed On: ▪ Amazon
             ▪ Goodreads
             ▪ Blog
             ▪ Audible
             ▪ Other

My Star Rating   ☆ ☆ ☆ ☆ ☆

TITLE:
....

AUTHOR:
....

DATE OF REVIEW:
....

Placed On: ▪ Amazon
             ▪ Goodreads
             ▪ Blog
             ▪ Audible
             ▪ Other

My Star Rating   ☆ ☆ ☆ ☆ ☆

MY AUGUST BOOK REVIEWS

TITLE:
....

AUTHOR:
....

DATE OF REVIEW:
....

Placed On:
- Amazon
- Goodreads
- Blog
- Audible
- Other

My Star Rating ☆ ☆ ☆ ☆ ☆

TITLE:
....

AUTHOR:
....

DATE OF REVIEW:
....

Placed On:
- Amazon
- Goodreads
- Blog
- Audible
- Other

My Star Rating ☆ ☆ ☆ ☆ ☆

MY AUGUST BOOK REVIEWS

TITLE:
....

AUTHOR:
....

DATE OF REVIEW:
....

Placed On:
- Amazon
- Goodreads
- Blog
- Audible
- Other

My Star Rating ☆ ☆ ☆ ☆ ☆

TITLE:
....

AUTHOR:
....

DATE OF REVIEW:
....

Placed On:
- Amazon
- Goodreads
- Blog
- Audible
- Other

My Star Rating ☆ ☆ ☆ ☆ ☆

MY AUGUST BOOK REVIEWS

TITLE:
....

AUTHOR:
....

DATE OF REVIEW:
....

Placed On: ▪ Amazon
             ▪ Goodreads
             ▪ Blog
             ▪ Audible
             ▪ Other

My Star Rating   ☆ ☆ ☆ ☆ ☆

TITLE:
....

AUTHOR:
....

DATE OF REVIEW:
....

Placed On: ▪ Amazon
             ▪ Goodreads
             ▪ Blog
             ▪ Audible
             ▪ Other

My Star Rating   ☆ ☆ ☆ ☆ ☆

After some discussion it was decided that a glass or two of wine at book club was acceptable. This may not have been the wisest decision.

"When did the worried well turn into the worried sick"
Hildegarde Boneforte (The Hon.)

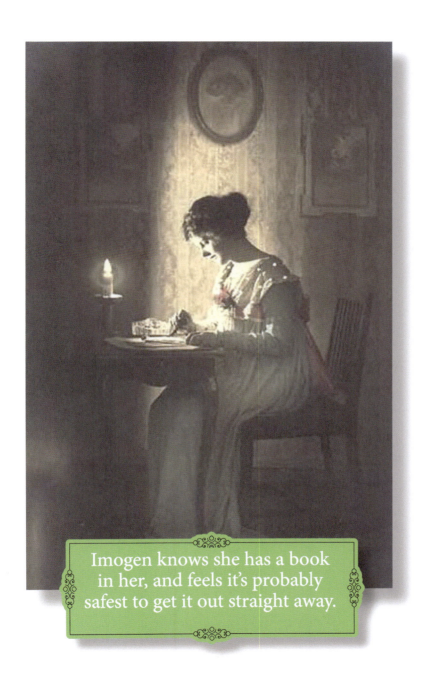

Imogen knows she has a book in her, and feels it's probably safest to get it out straight away.

BOOKS DURING SEPTEMBER

TITLE:
....

AUTHOR:
....

Book   Ebook   Audio   Series   Standalone   New Author

✎ MY THOUGHTS ✎

....
....
....
....
....
....
....
....
....
....
....
....
....
....
....
....
....
....
....
....
....
....

BOOKS DURING SEPTEMBER

TITLE: ....

AUTHOR: ....

Book   Ebook   Audio   Series   Standalone   New Author

✥ MY THOUGHTS ✥

BOOKS DURING SEPTEMBER

TITLE:
....
AUTHOR:
....

Book ▫ Ebook ▫ Audio ▫ Series ▫ Standalone ▫ New Author ▫

✦ MY THOUGHTS ✦

....
....
....
....
....
....
....
....
....
....
....
....
....
....
....
....
....
....
....
....
....
....
....
....
....

BOOKS DURING SEPTEMBER

TITLE:
....

AUTHOR:
....

Book   Ebook   Audio   Series   Standalone   New Author

❦ MY THOUGHTS ❦

BOOKS DURING SEPTEMBER

TITLE:
....

AUTHOR:
....

Book   Ebook   Audio   Series   Standalone   New Author

MY THOUGHTS

....
....
....
....
....
....
....
....
....
....
....
....
....
....
....
....
....
....
....
....
....
....
....
....

BOOKS DURING SEPTEMBER

TITLE:

AUTHOR:

Book   Ebook   Audio   Series   Standalone   New Author

❧ MY THOUGHTS ❧

BOOKS DURING SEPTEMBER

TITLE:
....
AUTHOR:
....

Book ▪ Ebook ▪ Audio ▪ Series ▪ Standalone ▪ New Author

❦ MY THOUGHTS ❦

BOOKS DURING SEPTEMBER

TITLE:

AUTHOR:

Book   Ebook   Audio   Series   Standalone   New Author

✒ MY THOUGHTS ✒

MY SEPTEMBER BOOK REVIEWS

TITLE:
....

AUTHOR:
....

DATE OF REVIEW:
....

Placed On: ▪ Amazon
     ▪ Goodreads
     ▪ Blog
     ▪ Audible
     ▪ Other

My Star Rating ☆ ☆ ☆ ☆ ☆

TITLE:
....

AUTHOR:
....

DATE OF REVIEW:
....

Placed On: ▪ Amazon
     ▪ Goodreads
     ▪ Blog
     ▪ Audible
     ▪ Other

My Star Rating ☆ ☆ ☆ ☆ ☆

MY SEPTEMBER BOOK REVIEWS

TITLE:
....

AUTHOR:
....

DATE OF REVIEW:
....

Placed On:	☐ Amazon
	☐ Goodreads
	☐ Blog
	☐ Audible
	☐ Other

My Star Rating	☆ ☆ ☆ ☆ ☆

TITLE:
....

AUTHOR:
....

DATE OF REVIEW:
....

Placed On:	☐ Amazon
	☐ Goodreads
	☐ Blog
	☐ Audible
	☐ Other

My Star Rating	☆ ☆ ☆ ☆ ☆

MY SEPTEMBER BOOK REVIEWS

TITLE:
....

AUTHOR:
....

DATE OF REVIEW:
....

Placed On:
- Amazon
- Goodreads
- Blog
- Audible
- Other

My Star Rating ☆ ☆ ☆ ☆ ☆

TITLE:
....

AUTHOR:
....

DATE OF REVIEW:
....

Placed On:
- Amazon
- Goodreads
- Blog
- Audible
- Other

My Star Rating ☆ ☆ ☆ ☆ ☆

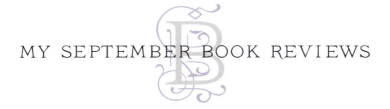

MY SEPTEMBER BOOK REVIEWS

TITLE:
....

AUTHOR:
....

DATE OF REVIEW:
....

Placed On: ☐ Amazon
             ☐ Goodreads
             ☐ Blog
             ☐ Audible
             ☐ Other

My Star Rating   ☆ ☆ ☆ ☆ ☆

TITLE:
....

AUTHOR:
....

DATE OF REVIEW:
....

Placed On: ☐ Amazon
             ☐ Goodreads
             ☐ Blog
             ☐ Audible
             ☐ Other

My Star Rating   ☆ ☆ ☆ ☆ ☆

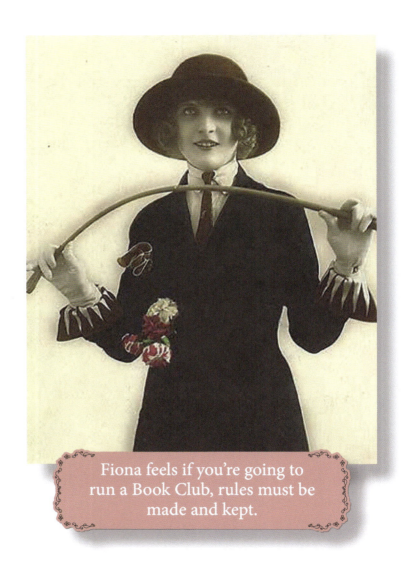

Fiona feels if you're going to run a Book Club, rules must be made and kept.

"A Vintage Lady always carries a safety pin
about her person, and is thus equipped to deal with
whatever eventuality may arise be it costume malfunction
or uninvited hand on the knee."
Hildegarde Boneforte (The Hon.)

Every best seller starts with a single line, and as soon as Drucilla can think of one, she'll be well away.

BOOKS DURING OCTOBER

TITLE:
....

AUTHOR:
....

Book   Ebook   Audio   Series   Standalone   New Author

MY THOUGHTS

BOOKS DURING OCTOBER

TITLE: ....

AUTHOR: ....

Book ▫ Ebook ▫ Audio ▫ Series ▫ Standalone ▫ New Author ▫

✎ MY THOUGHTS ✎

BOOKS DURING OCTOBER

TITLE:
....

AUTHOR:
....

Book   Ebook   Audio   Series   Standalone   New Author

⊸ MY THOUGHTS ⊷

....
....
....
....
....
....
....
....
....
....
....
....
....
....
....
....
....
....
....
....
....
....
....

BOOKS DURING OCTOBER

TITLE:

AUTHOR:

Book ▢ Ebook ▢ Audio ▢ Series ▢ Standalone ▢ New Author ▢

~ MY THOUGHTS ~

BOOKS DURING OCTOBER

TITLE:
....

AUTHOR:
....

Book ▪ Ebook ▪ Audio ▪ Series ▪ Standalone ▪ New Author

❦ MY THOUGHTS ❦

BOOKS DURING OCTOBER

TITLE:

AUTHOR:

Book   Ebook   Audio   Series   Standalone   New Author

✑ MY THOUGHTS ✑

BOOKS DURING OCTOBER

TITLE:
....

AUTHOR:
....

Book   Ebook   Audio   Series   Standalone   New Author

~ MY THOUGHTS ~

BOOKS DURING OCTOBER

TITLE:

AUTHOR:

Book   Ebook   Audio   Series   Standalone   New Author

MY THOUGHTS

MY OCTOBER BOOK REVIEWS

TITLE:
....

AUTHOR:
....

DATE OF REVIEW:
....

Placed On:
- Amazon
- Goodreads
- Blog
- Audible
- Other

My Star Rating   ☆ ☆ ☆ ☆ ☆

TITLE:
....

AUTHOR:
....

DATE OF REVIEW:
....

Placed On:
- Amazon
- Goodreads
- Blog
- Audible
- Other

My Star Rating   ☆ ☆ ☆ ☆ ☆

MY OCTOBER BOOK REVIEWS

TITLE:
....

AUTHOR:
....

DATE OF REVIEW:
....

Placed On: ☐ Amazon
            ☐ Goodreads
            ☐ Blog
            ☐ Audible
            ☐ Other

My Star Rating   ☆ ☆ ☆ ☆ ☆

TITLE:
....

AUTHOR:
....

DATE OF REVIEW:
....

Placed On: ☐ Amazon
            ☐ Goodreads
            ☐ Blog
            ☐ Audible
            ☐ Other

My Star Rating   ☆ ☆ ☆ ☆ ☆

MY OCTOBER BOOK REVIEWS

TITLE:
....

AUTHOR:
....

DATE OF REVIEW:
....

Placed On:
- Amazon
- Goodreads
- Blog
- Audible
- Other

My Star Rating   ☆ ☆ ☆ ☆ ☆

TITLE:
....

AUTHOR:
....

DATE OF REVIEW:
....

Placed On:
- Amazon
- Goodreads
- Blog
- Audible
- Other

My Star Rating   ☆ ☆ ☆ ☆ ☆

MY OCTOBER BOOK REVIEWS

TITLE:
....

AUTHOR:
....

DATE OF REVIEW:
....

Placed On:
☐ Amazon
☐ Goodreads
☐ Blog
☐ Audible
☐ Other

My Star Rating   ☆ ☆ ☆ ☆ ☆

TITLE:
....

AUTHOR:
....

DATE OF REVIEW:
....

Placed On:
☐ Amazon
☐ Goodreads
☐ Blog
☐ Audible
☐ Other

My Star Rating   ☆ ☆ ☆ ☆ ☆

Earnestine has found an embossed leather cover can cover a multitude of sins.

Myrtle didn't deal well with sad endings.

"It is an unfortunate fact that as one matures, eye lashes have a tendency to migrate to the chin."
Hildegarde Boneforte (The Hon.)

BOOKS DURING NOVEMBER

TITLE:
....

AUTHOR:
....

Book ▪ Ebook ▪ Audio ▪ Series ▪ Standalone ▪ New Author

⇜ MY THOUGHTS ⇝

BOOKS DURING NOVEMBER

TITLE:

AUTHOR:

Book   Ebook   Audio   Series   Standalone   New Author

MY THOUGHTS

BOOKS DURING NOVEMBER

TITLE:
....

AUTHOR:
....

Book ▪ Ebook ▪ Audio ▪ Series ▪ Standalone ▪ New Author

⇜ MY THOUGHTS ⇝

BOOKS DURING NOVEMBER

TITLE:

AUTHOR:

Book   Ebook   Audio   Series   Standalone   New Author

MY THOUGHTS

BOOKS DURING NOVEMBER

TITLE:
....

AUTHOR:
....

Book ▪ Ebook ▪ Audio ▪ Series ▪ Standalone ▪ New Author

⇜ MY THOUGHTS ⇝

BOOKS DURING NOVEMBER

TITLE:
....

AUTHOR:
....

Book   Ebook   Audio   Series   Standalone   New Author

~ MY THOUGHTS ~

BOOKS DURING NOVEMBER

TITLE:
....
AUTHOR:
....

Book   Ebook   Audio   Series   Standalone   New Author

✧ MY THOUGHTS ✧

....
....
....
....
....
....
....
....
....
....
....
....
....
....
....
....
....
....
....
....
....

BOOKS DURING NOVEMBER

TITLE:

AUTHOR:

Book ☐ Ebook ☐ Audio ☐ Series ☐ Standalone ☐ New Author ☐

✥ MY THOUGHTS ✥

MY NOVEMBER BOOK REVIEWS

TITLE:
....

AUTHOR:
....

DATE OF REVIEW:
....

Placed On:
- Amazon
- Goodreads
- Blog
- Audible
- Other

My Star Rating ☆ ☆ ☆ ☆ ☆

TITLE:
....

AUTHOR:
....

DATE OF REVIEW:
....

Placed On:
- Amazon
- Goodreads
- Blog
- Audible
- Other

My Star Rating ☆ ☆ ☆ ☆ ☆

MY NOVEMBER BOOK REVIEWS

TITLE:
....

AUTHOR:
....

DATE OF REVIEW:
....

Placed On: ☐ Amazon
             ☐ Goodreads
             ☐ Blog
             ☐ Audible
             ☐ Other

My Star Rating   ☆ ☆ ☆ ☆ ☆

TITLE:
....

AUTHOR:
....

DATE OF REVIEW:
....

Placed On: ☐ Amazon
             ☐ Goodreads
             ☐ Blog
             ☐ Audible
             ☐ Other

My Star Rating   ☆ ☆ ☆ ☆ ☆

MY NOVEMBER BOOK REVIEWS

TITLE:

AUTHOR:

DATE OF REVIEW:

Placed On: ▪ Amazon
 ▪ Goodreads
 ▪ Blog
 ▪ Audible
 ▪ Other

My Star Rating ☆ ☆ ☆ ☆ ☆

TITLE:

AUTHOR:

DATE OF REVIEW:

Placed On: ▪ Amazon
 ▪ Goodreads
 ▪ Blog
 ▪ Audible
 ▪ Other

My Star Rating ☆ ☆ ☆ ☆ ☆

MY NOVEMBER BOOK REVIEWS

TITLE:
....

AUTHOR:
....

DATE OF REVIEW:
....

Placed On:
- Amazon
- Goodreads
- Blog
- Audible
- Other

My Star Rating ☆ ☆ ☆ ☆ ☆

TITLE:
....

AUTHOR:
....

DATE OF REVIEW:
....

Placed On:
- Amazon
- Goodreads
- Blog
- Audible
- Other

My Star Rating ☆ ☆ ☆ ☆ ☆

Cecil and Celia are hosting book club this month. They always make a bit of a song and dance about it.

"Some men find an intelligent woman intimidating. Good!"

Hildegarde Boneforte (The Hon.)

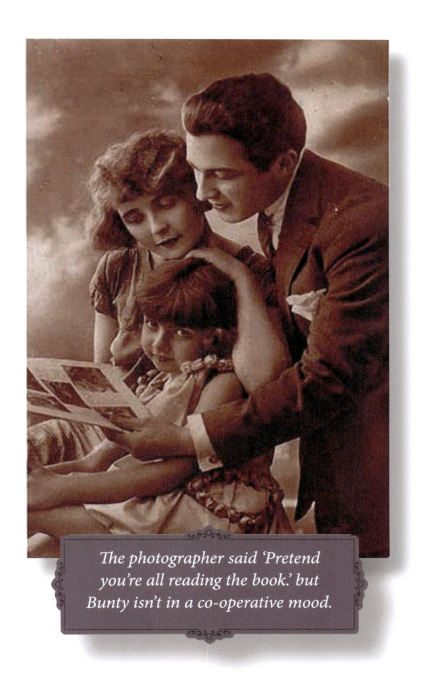

The photographer said 'Pretend you're all reading the book.' but Bunty isn't in a co-operative mood.

BOOKS DURING DECEMBER

TITLE:
....
AUTHOR:
....

Book ▪ Ebook ▪ Audio ▪ Series ▪ Standalone ▪ New Author

~ MY THOUGHTS ~

....
....
....
....
....
....
....
....
....
....
....
....
....
....
....
....
....
....
....
....
....
....
....
....

BOOKS DURING DECEMBER

TITLE:
....

AUTHOR:
....

Book ▪ Ebook ▪ Audio ▪ Series ▪ Standalone ▪ New Author ▪

❧ MY THOUGHTS ☙

BOOKS DURING DECEMBER

TITLE:
....
AUTHOR:
....

Book ▫   Ebook ▫   Audio ▫   Series ▫   Standalone ▫   New Author

⁓ MY THOUGHTS ⁓

BOOKS DURING DECEMBER

TITLE:
....
AUTHOR:
....

Book ▪ Ebook ▪ Audio ▪ Series ▪ Standalone ▪ New Author

✎ MY THOUGHTS ✎

BOOKS DURING DECEMBER

TITLE:
....

AUTHOR:
....

Book ▪ Ebook ▪ Audio ▪ Series ▪ Standalone ▪ New Author

∼ MY THOUGHTS ∼

BOOKS DURING DECEMBER

TITLE:
....

AUTHOR:
....

Book ▪ Ebook ▪ Audio ▪ Series ▪ Standalone ▪ New Author ▪

✥ MY THOUGHTS ✥

BOOKS DURING DECEMBER

TITLE:
....

AUTHOR:
....

Book ▪ Ebook ▪ Audio ▪ Series ▪ Standalone ▪ New Author ▪

✎ MY THOUGHTS ✎

....
....
....
....
....
....
....
....
....
....
....
....
....
....
....
....
....
....
....
....
....
....
....

BOOKS DURING DECEMBER

TITLE:
....

AUTHOR:
....

Book ▪ Ebook ▪ Audio ▪ Series ▪ Standalone ▪ New Author ▪

~ MY THOUGHTS ~

MY DECEMBER BOOK REVIEWS

TITLE:
....
AUTHOR:
....
DATE OF REVIEW:
....

Placed On:　　☐ Amazon
　　　　　　　☐ Goodreads
　　　　　　　☐ Blog
　　　　　　　☐ Audible
　　　　　　　☐ Other

My Star Rating　☆ ☆ ☆ ☆ ☆

TITLE:
....
AUTHOR:
....
DATE OF REVIEW:
....

Placed On:　　☐ Amazon
　　　　　　　☐ Goodreads
　　　　　　　☐ Blog
　　　　　　　☐ Audible
　　　　　　　☐ Other

My Star Rating　☆ ☆ ☆ ☆ ☆

MY DECEMBER BOOK REVIEWS

TITLE:
....

AUTHOR:
....

DATE OF REVIEW:
....

Placed On:
- Amazon
- Goodreads
- Blog
- Audible
- Other

My Star Rating   ☆ ☆ ☆ ☆ ☆

TITLE:
....

AUTHOR:
....

DATE OF REVIEW:
....

Placed On:
- Amazon
- Goodreads
- Blog
- Audible
- Other

My Star Rating   ☆ ☆ ☆ ☆ ☆

MY DECEMBER BOOK REVIEWS

TITLE:
....

AUTHOR:
....

DATE OF REVIEW:
....

Placed On: ▪ Amazon
             ▪ Goodreads
             ▪ Blog
             ▪ Audible
             ▪ Other

My Star Rating   ☆ ☆ ☆ ☆ ☆

TITLE:
....

AUTHOR:
....

DATE OF REVIEW:
....

Placed On: ▪ Amazon
             ▪ Goodreads
             ▪ Blog
             ▪ Audible
             ▪ Other

My Star Rating   ☆ ☆ ☆ ☆ ☆

MY DECEMBER BOOK REVIEWS

TITLE:
....

AUTHOR:
....

DATE OF REVIEW:
....

Placed On:
- Amazon
- Goodreads
- Blog
- Audible
- Other

My Star Rating ☆ ☆ ☆ ☆ ☆

TITLE:
....

AUTHOR:
....

DATE OF REVIEW:
....

Placed On:
- Amazon
- Goodreads
- Blog
- Audible
- Other

My Star Rating ☆ ☆ ☆ ☆ ☆

NOTES

....
....
....
....
....
....
....
....
....
....
....
....
....
....
....
....
....
....
....
....
....
....
....
....

*"Giving you peace of mind is one thing,
giving you a piece of mine, quite another."*
Hildegarde Boneforte (The Hon.)

NOTES

NOTES

THE
VINTAGE
LADIES

Hello Fellow Book Lover,

I very much hope you've enjoyed using the Book Lovers Log. However if there was anything which made you put your hands to your head and shriek because we've missed something , do let me know. I'm always happy to include as many suggestions, additions or amendments as I possibly can. If on the other hand you've loved everything about the Log, shout out about that too – nothing puts a spring in my step like a happy customer.

I am hesitant to ask a favour, but as Hildegarde so succinctly says,'She who fails to ask, fails to gain!'. So if you've enjoyed the Log, and have a spare moment, a swift review on Amazon, Goodreads or indeed a local brick wall would be hugely appreciated.

Should you feel there are others in your life who might enjoy the Vintage Ladies and the wisdom of Hildegarde, we're constantly working on new products, and if you let me have your email and ask to be kept up to date it would be my great pleasure to do so. In the meantime, may you always have a book to hand, and several others lined up waiting.

Very best wishes

Marilyn

marilyn@createcommunication.co.uk

Cedric's published his first novel, and says he wants Ruby's honest opinion. Ruby feels it wouldn't be kind to give it.

Printed in Great Britain
by Amazon